Basic
Troubleshooting For
A Kindle Voyage

Basic Troubleshooting

For A Kindle Voyage

Table of Contents

Screen Issues

Charging Issues

Buy & Downloading

Content

Downloading Issues

Wireless Issues

Forgot Kindle Passcode

Book Won't Open

This Book Will be also available in paperback on Amazon

Basic troubleshooting for the Kindle Voyage.

Hello too all the millions of Amazon Kindle users. Kindle is a great product but sometimes has it problems. So I made this e book to make it easier for all the Kindle users out there to troubleshoot their device before calling Amazon Kindle support which does an awesome job but whose wants to spend a lot of time on the phone. This e book will cover the Kindle Voyage e-reader. This e book will cover screen issues, wireless issues, and apps issues and much more so let's get started.

A Little Information to Know

- Before doing any trouble shooting on your devices make sure the battery is charged up to at least 40% or more.

- The number to Kindle support is 1-866-321-8851

- Before resetting your device to factory default settings contact Kindle support so they can get information off the device in case further troubleshooting is needed.

  When doing a hard reset of the device hold the power button for at least 30 – 45 seconds to make sure the device resets.

- You want to make sure your Kindle always has the most recent software updates. Use the help pages on www.amazon.com to see if you have the most recent updates.

- With some wireless issues make sure you have the correct password sometimes they can be enter wrong so just double check to be sure. If you see a white x next to the wife symbol that means that there is an issue with your router. Kindle support cannot troubleshoot routers you much contact the company or person who install it for you to check the settings in the router.

Screen Issues

Device has an image stuck on the screen or lines running across or up and down the screen this could mean screen damaged that can't be fixed

Troubleshooting

A. Try too hard reset the device by pressing the power button for 30-45 seconds then releasing the button with the device unplug for the charger then let the device reboot and see if you still have the issue.

B. Try too hard reset the device by pressing the power button for 30-45 seconds then releasing the button with the device plug into the charger then let the device reboot and see if you still have the issue.

C. Make sure your device is up to date on its software. From the home screen hit Menu and then settings, on the bottom right of the screen you will see the Kindle version your device has. Check on

www.amazon.com on the help pages to make sure you have the most updated software.

D. If this does not fix your issue contact Kindle Support. 1-866-321-8851.

Charging Issues

Device will not hold a charge or shows no signs of charging.

Troubleshooting

Note: If you're using a power adapter to charge your Kindle, make sure the USB cable that came with your device is securely connected to the power adapter. Sometimes battery charging issues can be caused by a faulty or damaged USB cable or power adapter.

A.   Put your Kindle into sleep mode when you're finished reading. To put your Kindle into sleep mode and conserve battery life, press the Power button on your device.

B.   Turn off your wireless connection. Your Kindle uses more battery power when connected to a Wi-Fi or 3G network. To turn off your wireless connection, tap the Menu icon, tap Settings, and then select ON next to Airplane Mode.

C. Charge your Kindle with a compatible power adapter. While you can charge your Kindle with the supplied USB cable, some computers and older keyboards may not provide enough power to fully charge the device. With a compatible power adapter sold separately, your Kindle charges in less than six hours.

D. Restart your Kindle. Disconnect the device from the USB cable, and then press and hold the Power button for 7 seconds. In the Power dialog box that appears, tap Restart. After your Kindle restarts, connect the USB cable to your Kindle and your computer or a compatible power adapter to verify if you're Kindle is charging.

E. If this does not fix your issue contact Kindle Support. 1-866-321-8851.

Buy & Download Kindle Content

How to buy content on your device?

Troubleshooting

If your Kindle includes 3G, you are connected automatically. You can buy and download Kindle content using 3G, but you can download faster if you connect to a Wi-Fi network.

After you purchase Kindle content, it automatically downloads to your device. The content is also stored in the Cloud so you can download it to other Kindle devices or Kindle reading apps registered to the same account.

A. **To visit the Kindle Store, tap the Kindle Store of Amazon shopping cart icon.**

B. **When you are ready to purchase a title, tap the Buy button.**

C. **To subscribe to a newspaper or magazine, tap Subscribe now.**

D. Tap Try a Sample to download the beginning of the book for free.

E. Tap the Home icon for home icon to view and open your new Kindle content.

F. To see a video of this click on the link below

https://www.amazon.com/gp/help/customer/display.html?nodeId=201733660

Downloading Issues

Troubleshooting

Books or purchases does not show up on your device.

A. Make sure your order has when through and it is paid for. Orders can be put into a pending status which can take up to 4 hours to clear. Also make sure you are purchasing the items on the correct account. Customers with multiple accounts can purchases item on the account their devices are not register too which they cannot get the books onto their devices.

B. Make sure your device has a good connection where your purchases can download.

C. You can go and log on to your account at www.amazon.com and go to Manage Your Kindle and see if the purchase show up in your library and send it to your device from there.

D. Try too hard reset the device by pressing the power button for 30-45 seconds then releasing the button then let the device reboot and see if you still have the issue.

E. Make sure your device is up to date on its software. From the home screen hit Menu and then settings, on the bottom right of the screen you will see the Kindle version your device has. Check on www.amazon.com on the help pages to make sure you have the most updated software.

F. If this does not fix your issue contact Kindle Support. 1-866-321-8851.

Wireless Issues

If you device cannot connect to a wireless network.

Troubleshooting

A. If you have difficulty connecting to the Kindle store or other wireless resources

on your Kindle, make sure the wireless is turned on.

B. Make sure your network has a good connection Call your provider to make sure there is no outages in your area.

C. Try too hard reset the device by pressing the power button for 30-45 seconds then releasing the button then let the device reboot and see if you still have the issue.

D. Make sure your device is up to date on its software. From the home screen hit Menu and then settings, on the bottom right of the screen you will see the Kindle version your device has. Check on www.amazon.com on the help pages to make sure you have the most updated software.

E. De-register and the re-register the Kindle then do a hard reset then let the device reboot and try to connect to your network. If you still have the issue. Go to a local place that providers free Wi-Fi and see if you can connect there to rule out if there is anything wrong with your connection at home or work.

F. Reset to factory Default but not recommended until you contact Kindle support so they can get information off the device in case further troubleshooting is needed. 1-866-321-8851.

Forgot Kindle Passcode

Troubleshooting

<u>Important:</u> Resetting your Kindle will remove your personal information (including your lock screen passcode), Amazon account information, and downloaded content. Any content you purchased from Amazon is automatically saved to the Cloud. You can download that content when you register your Kindle to your account again.

A. Tap the passcode field to bring up the onscreen keyboard.

B. Type 111222777, and then tap OK. Your Kindle will restart.

C. To use you're Kindle again, you'll need to connect to a wireless network and register your Kindle.

Book Won't Open

Your book will not open after you have tap on it.

Before you perform these steps, make sure that your Kindle is connected to a wireless network. To learn more, go to Connect to Wi-Fi.

There may have been an error with downloading the book. Remove the title from your device, restart your device, and then download the book again.

A. From Home, tap the On Device tab.

B. Press and hold the title of the Kindle book to remove, and then tap Delete This Book.

C. Tap the Menu icon, tap Settings, tap the Menu icon again, and then tap Restart.

C. Tap the Cloud tab, and then tap the title of the Kindle book to download.

Reset Your Kindle

Note: Having trouble with your Kindle? Try to Restart Your Kindle without erasing content.

If you have any content that is not saved to your content library in the Cloud, be sure to transfer that content from your device to your computer via USB. For more information, go to Transfer from a Computer to Your Kindle.

You can't reset your Kindle if Parental Controls are set. If you forget your password, reset your Kindle by entering 111222777 as the Parental Controls password.

Important:

Resetting your Kindle will remove your personal information including your lock screen passcode, Amazon account information, and downloaded content. Any content you purchased from Amazon is automatically saved to the Cloud. You can download that content when you register your Kindle to your account again.

A. From Home, tap the Menu of menu icon, and then tap Settings.

B. Tap the Menu icon again, and then tap Reset Device. Your Kindle will restart.

C. To use your Kindle again, you'll need to connect to a wireless network and register your Kindle.